PARSLEY

PARSLEY

INTRODUCTION BY CHRIS INGRAM

southwater

This edition is published by Southwater

Southwater is an imprint of
Anness Publishing Limited
Hermes House
88–89 Blackfriars Road
London SE1 8HA
tel. 020 7401 2077
fax 020 7633 9499

Distributed in the UK by
The Manning Partnership
251–253 London Road East
Batheaston
Bath BA1 7RL
tel. 01225 852 727
fax 01225 852 852

Distributed in the USA by
Anness Publishing Inc.
27 West 20th Street
Suite 504
New York
NY 10011
tel. 212 807 6739
fax 212 807 6813

Distributed in Australia by
Sandstone Publishing
Unit 1
360 Norton Street
Leichhardt
New South Wales 2040
tel. 02 9560 7888
fax 02 9560 7488

© 1998, 2000 Anness Publishing Limited

1 3 5 7 9 10 8 6 4 2

Publisher Joanna Lorenz
Senior Cookery Editor Linda Fraser
Project Editor Margaret Malone
Designer Bill Mason
Illustrations Anna Koska

Photographers Karl Adamson, William Adams-Lingwood, Edward Allwright, Steve Baxter, James Duncan,
John Freeman, Michelle Garrett, Amanda Heywood, Don Last and Patrick McLeavey
Recipes Carla Capalbo, Maxine Clark, Andi Clevely, Christine France, Silvana Franco, Shirley Gill, Christine Ingram, Sue Maggs, Annie
Nichols, Katherine Richmond, Liz Trigg, Hilaire Walden, Laura Washburn and Steven Wheeler
Stylists Madeleine Brehaut, Hilary Guy, Blake Minton, Fiona Tillett and Elizabeth Wolf-Cohen

For all recipes, quantities are given in both metric and imperial measures and, where appropriate,
measures are also given in standard cups and spoons. Follow one set, but not a mixture,
because they are not interchangeable.

Previously published as *Cooking with Parsley*

Contents

$\mathcal{I}$NTRODUCTION

arsley has a very special place in the kitchen. Its mild unassuming flavor makes it the most versatile of herbs, adding a fine delicate flavor to an almost limitless number of savory dishes. Many herbs make their presence known in quite forceful ways. Cuisines, such as Italian, Turkish, and Thai, can be defined by their well-flavored, aromatic, or pungent herbs. Yet in all these cuisines, parsley is never forgotten. It may play a quieter, more modest role than its racier cousins, but it is still among the most widely used of herbs, appreciated for its subtle aromatic flavor and its vibrant color.

Parsley is native to southern Europe and was grown by the ancient Greeks, who used the herb for ceremonial and medicinal purposes as well as in salads and sauces. During the Isthmian games, victors would be crowned with wreaths of parsley and it was also laid upon the tombs of the dead. The Romans appreciated parsley as a food and introduced it to Britain where it flourished in the moderate climate.

Enthusiasm for parsley continued throughout the centuries. Since it could be grown so successfully in England it remained popular, unlike many of the herbs introduced from southern Europe. During the

Middle Ages, people would have grown the herb both for culinary and medicinal uses, as it was considered useful for a number of ailments. This reputation has found its way into stories too. Beatrix Potter's Peter Rabbit, after gorging himself on Mr McGregor's vegetable garden, finally nibbles on parsley to settle his stomach!

Indeed, parsley is one of the most nutritious of herbs. It is particularly high in carotene and vitamin C and contains useful amounts of potassium and calcium.

There are three main varieties of parsley. Curly parsley grows most successfully in northern climates and is the most popular in Britain. Flat leaf or Italian parsley is a less hardy plant than curly parsley and grows best in the warmer climates of southern Europe and the Middle East, where it is used in huge quantities. Parsley root, also called turnip-rooted or Hamburg parsley, although a member of the same family, is not used as an herb, but its roots are eaten as a vegetable.

The wonderful selection of recipes in this book, which concentrate on curly and flat leaf parsley, is a sound testimony to the versatility of this extraordinary herb. From soups and stocks to classic sauces and stuffings, this book serves as the perfect guide to the many culinary uses of this gentle herb.

Types of Parsley

CURLY PARSLEY

Sometimes called English parsley, this is the most common parsley and is certainly the most easily recognized. It has dark emerald green leaves that vary between very curled and softly curled. It has a good, fresh flavor and is particularly popular as a garnish.

FLAT LEAF PARSLEY

Also known as Italian parsley, this is the more favored parsley in European countries, particularly France, Spain, and Italy. It has pretty, rather lacy leaves, varying in color from pale to dark green. It has a more pronounced flavor that is pleasantly aromatic, giving salads and cooked dishes a distinct yet fresh flavor. It also makes a pretty garnish.

PARSLEY ROOT

This plant is grown mainly for its tapering root which looks rather like a thin parsnip and tastes like a cross between celery root and parsley. It is also referred to as Hamburg parsley and, as the name suggests, the plant is popular in Germany where it is used as a root vegetable.

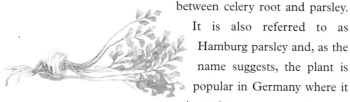

DRIED PARSLEY

Dried parsley is widely available, or you can dry your own very easily. Commercially-dried parsley has a reputation for having little or no flavor, although it is just about acceptable if there is no alternative and it is used shortly after opening. Store dried parsley in a cool dry place. Once opened, it should be used within 2–3 months. After that, dried parsley tastes much like dust.

FROZEN PARSLEY

Flat leaf and curly parsley are available frozen, or you can freeze your own parsley. Commercially frozen parsley comes in conveniently small containers and should be returned to the freezer once you have used what you need. Do not allow it to defrost and then re-freeze, as this could introduce bacteria as well as destroying flavor.

CHOPPED PARSLEY

Parsley is chopped both in cooking and for garnishing. It can be finely or coarsely chopped, either with a sharp knife or using an herb mill.

Flat leaf

Dried

Fresh chopped

Frozen chopped

Curly

$\mathcal{B}$ASIC $\mathcal{T}$ECHNIQUES

COOKING WITH PARSLEY

CHOPPING PARSLEY

To chop by hand, snip the leaves from the stalks and chop coarsely, bunching the leaves up against a knife. You can also use an herb mill or a coffee mill for small quantities of parsley, and a food processor for larger quantities.

FREEZING PARSLEY

Wash fresh parsley sprigs and shake dry carefully. Place in freezer bags, label, and freeze. For chopped parsley, place a tablespoon in ice cube trays and top up with water. The frozen cubes can be added directly to cooked dishes.

MAKING A BOUQUET GARNI

Take three parsley stalks, one small sprig of thyme, and one or two bay leaves and tie firmly with string. For a more aromatic bouquet garni, add a twist of orange or lemon peel, a piece of celery, and a sprig of marjoram.

DRYING PARSLEY

Use parsley that is absolutely fresh. Tie into bundles and hang from a rack in a warm, dry room, not exceeding 86°F. Leave for a week, until the leaves are crisp and dry. To keep the parsley dust-free, place brown paper bags over the tops of the bunches, leaving the bottom open to allow air to circulate. Once completely dry, strip the leaves from the stem and place in a jar. Close tightly and check the next day for condensation, which indicates that the leaves are not completely dry. If this is the case, place the parsley on a rack lined with cheesecloth and leave in a warm room for 24 hours more. Store dried parsley in airtight dark glass or pottery jars.

GROWING YOUR OWN PARSLEY

Parsley will grow happily in a warm place outside the kitchen door, or on the windowsill. It needs plenty of sun, and on warm days should be kept watered or the plant will wither and die. To grow your own parsley, soak the seeds overnight and then sow directly into pots or into the earth in early spring. The soil must be watered regularly with a fine spray during germination. Once the seedlings are big enough to handle, they should be thinned until the plants are about 8 inches apart. Parsley seeds are notoriously slow to germinate and a quicker, albeit less satisfying, course would be to buy small plants from your local nursery. These can be kept indoors or outside, in earthenware pots, hanging baskets, or in a pretty windowsill arrangement.

PARSLEY, SAGE AND THYME OIL

This pleasantly herb-flavored oil is perfect for salad greens and for stir-fries.

Pour $2\frac{1}{2}$ cups sunflower oil into a sterilized jar and add $\frac{1}{2}$ cup chopped fresh parsley, 2 tablespoons chopped fresh sage, and $\frac{1}{4}$ cup chopped fresh thyme. Cover and let stand at room temperature for 1 week. Stir or shake occasionally during that time. Strain the oil through a strainer lined with cheesecloth into a sterilized pitcher and then decant into sterilized bottles, discarding the used herbs. Add a fresh sprig of parsley or thyme for decoration, if desired. Seal the jar carefully, label, and store in a cool place. Use within 6 months. Makes $2\frac{1}{2}$ cups.

HOW TO MAKE PARSLEY SAUCE

Parsley sauce is a classic recipe that you will find yourself using for all sorts of dishes. It's essential with white fish, root vegetables, and many green vegetables. It's wonderful with fava beans and is the classic accompaniment to ham and gammon. Curly parsley is the more commonly used variety for this traditional English sauce, but flat leaf parsley is excellent, giving a more distinct, aromatic flavor.

Melt 3 tablespoons butter in a saucepan. Add 2 tablespoons all-purpose flour and cook gently for 1 minute, stirring constantly.

Gradually stir in 1³/₄ cups milk, beating until smooth after each addition, to make a smooth sauce. Cook very gently for about 1 minute.

Stir in 3 tablespoons finely chopped fresh parsley and season to taste. For a richer parsley sauce, add 1 tablespoon light cream.

PARSLEY KNOW-HOW

- *Most of the flavor of parsley is in the stalks: use these for making stocks and bouquets garnis.*
- *The more densely curled the parsley, the better it is for cooking. Flat leaf parsley is always chopped before being added to dishes.*

- *In sauces, add parsley at the last minute so that it simply heats through. As a general rule, parsley should only be heated, not cooked.*
- *An exception to the above is to deep-fry sprigs of parsley and serve them as a fantastic starter or garnish.*

- *Parsley is an essential ingredient in French fines herbes. Chop finely with chervil, chives, and tarragon and use for omelets, in stuffings, and as a garnish for mushrooms.*

SIMPLE PARSLEY IDEAS

Green sauce: This is a popular Mediterranean sauce that tastes particularly good with fish. Place 1$\frac{1}{2}$ cups fresh flat leaf parsley, 1 garlic clove, and 2 shallots in a food processor. Soak a slice of day-old bread in water, squeeze dry, and add to the bowl with 2 teaspoons rinsed capers and 2 tablespoons white wine vinegar. Add 5 tablespoons olive oil, season, and process until well combined but not completely smooth. Pour into a bowl, cover, and let infuse for 1 hour before serving.

Gremolata: This Italian flavoring is made from very finely chopped lemon or orange rind, garlic, and parsley. It is traditionally sprinkled over Osso Buco, but can be used as a garnish for any rich, braised meat dishes.

Parsley butter: Mash $\frac{1}{2}$ cup softened sweet butter and blend with $\frac{1}{2}$ crushed garlic clove, 1 tablespoon lemon juice, and 3 tablespoons chopped fresh parsley. Shape into a log and roll up in waxed paper. Chill and slice as required. Alternatively, chill the butter slightly and roll out between sheets of waxed paper. Cut into shapes and chill until ready to serve.

Parsley dressing: Place 4 tablespoons olive oil, 2 tablespoons sunflower oil, 1 tablespoon lemon juice, and 3 tablespoons chopped fresh parsley in a screw-top jar. Add a pinch of sugar and seasoning, replace the lid, and shake well.

Parsley mayonnaise: Stir $\frac{1}{2}$ cup finely chopped flat leaf parsley into 1 cup homemade or store-bought mayonnaise.

Parsley stuffing: For a stuffing for lamb, turkey, or chicken: fry 2–3 snipped bacon slices with 1 finely chopped onion in a little butter and/or oil. Mix with 1$\frac{1}{2}$–2 cups fresh bread crumbs and 1 diced apple. Add 3 tablespoons chopped fresh parsley and season well. Moisten with lemon juice and a little chicken stock if necessary.

Persillade: Very finely chop 1$\frac{1}{2}$ cups fresh flat leaf parsley and mix with 2 very finely chopped shallots or 2 very finely chopped garlic cloves. Add a good pinch of salt and mix well. Stir into casseroles and fish and poultry dishes just before serving for a fresh Provençal flavor.

Soups, Starters, and Snacks

Make the most of parsley for all your starters.
Parsley adds a fresh, country-style flavor to all
sorts of dishes—whether old-fashioned favorites
or up-to-the-minute soups and snacks.

ITALIAN BEAN AND PARSLEY SOUP

Italian flat leaf parsley adds a fresh, aromatic flavor to this well-flavored and hearty soup.

Serves 6

1 cup dried navy beans,
    soaked overnight

7½ cups chicken stock or water

1 cup pasta shells

4 tablespoons olive oil, plus extra,
    to serve

2 garlic cloves, crushed

4 tablespoons chopped fresh flat leaf
    parsley

salt and freshly ground black pepper

COOK'S TIP

Use medium-size pasta shells or shapes for this recipe. If using fresh pasta, simmer for just 5–6 minutes until tender.

Drain the beans and place in a large saucepan with the stock or water. Bring to a boil, boil rapidly for 10 minutes, then lower the heat, and simmer, half-covered, for 2–2½ hours, until the beans are tender. Spoon half of the beans and a little of their cooking liquid into a blender or food processor and process until smooth. Stir back into the remaining beans in the pan.

Add the pasta and simmer gently for 15 minutes, until the pasta is tender, adding a little extra water or stock if the soup seems too thick.

Heat the oil in a small pan and fry the garlic until golden. Stir into the soup with the parsley and season well with salt and pepper. Ladle into warm soup bowls and drizzle each with a little extra olive oil.

GARBANZO BEAN AND PARSLEY SOUP

This tasty soup, served with a tangy lemon garnish, comes from Morocco, where parsley is a favorite ingredient. If possible, use flat leaf parsley.

Serves 6

1¼ cups garbanzo beans, soaked overnight

1 small onion

1½ cups fresh flat leaf parsley

2 tablespoons olive and sunflower oil, mixed

5 cups chicken stock

juice of ½ lemon

salt and freshly ground black pepper

lemon wedges and finely pared strips of rind, to garnish

crusty bread, to serve

Drain the garbanzo beans and rinse under cold water. Cook them in boiling water for 1–1½ hours, until tender. Drain and peel (see Cook's Tip).

Place the onion and flat leaf parsley in a blender or food processor and process until finely chopped. Alternatively, chop each very finely and combine. Heat the olive and sunflower oils in a saucepan or flameproof casserole and fry the onion mixture for 3–4 minutes over low heat, until the onion is slightly softened. Add the garbanzo beans, cook gently for 1–2 minutes, and then add the stock. Season well with salt and pepper. Bring the soup to a boil, then cover, and simmer for 20 minutes, until the garbanzo beans are very tender.

Allow the soup to cool a little and then part-purée in a blender or food processor, or mash with a fork, so that the soup is thick but still chunky.

Return the soup to a clean pan, add the lemon juice, and adjust the seasoning if necessary. Heat gently and then serve garnished with lemon wedges and finely pared rind, and accompanied by crusty bread.

COOK'S TIP

Garbanzo beans blend better in soups and other dishes if you rub off the outer skin. Although this will take you some time, it is worth the effort, as the soup will be smoother.

CEP SOUP WITH PARSLEY CROÛTONS

The little parsley croûtons add a mild, herb flavor to this delicious and unusual soup.

Serves 4

4 tablespoons butter

2 onions, finely chopped

1 garlic clove

3 cups sliced fresh ceps or
   button mushrooms

5 tablespoons dry white wine

3¾ cups boiling chicken stock

4 ounces mealy potatoes, peeled
   and diced

1 fresh thyme sprig

1 tablespoon lemon juice

salt and freshly ground black pepper

For the parsley croûtons

4 tablespoons butter

3 slices day-old bread, cut into
   1-inch fingers

3 tablespoons finely chopped
   fresh parsley

Melt the butter in a large saucepan and fry the onions for 4–5 minutes, until lightly browned. Add the garlic, mushrooms, and wine, stir briefly, then add the stock, potatoes, and thyme. Simmer gently for 45 minutes.

Pour the soup into a blender or food processor and process briefly so that pieces of mushroom are left intact. Transfer the soup to a clean pan, add the lemon juice, and season to taste.

Make the croûtons. Melt the butter in a large skillet and add the fingers of bread. Fry for 2–3 minutes, until golden, and then stir in the parsley. Ladle the soup into warm soup bowls, add the parsley croûtons, and serve immediately.

SALSA VERDE

This is a classic salsa, made with chilies, onions, and plenty of fresh parsley.

Serves 4

2–4 green chilies, seeded

8 scallions, trimmed and halved

2 garlic cloves, halved

⅓ cup salted capers

fresh tarragon sprig

1½ cups fresh parsley

grated rind and juice of 1 lime

6 tablespoons olive oil

about 1 tablespoon green Tabasco
    sauce, to taste

freshly ground black pepper

COOK'S TIP

*If you can only find capers
pickled in vinegar, rinse well in
cold water before using.*

Place the chilies, scallions, and garlic in a blender or food processor and process briefly until the ingredients are roughly chopped. Rub the excess salt off the capers, but do not rinse them. Add the capers to the chili and onion mixture, together with the tarragon and parsley. Process again until finely chopped.

Transfer the mixture to a small bowl and stir in the lime rind and juice and olive oil. Stir briefly to mix. Add the green Tabasco sauce and black pepper. Chill in the fridge until ready to serve, but do not prepare more than 8 hours in advance.

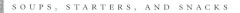

BROILED PARSLEY MUSSELS

This is a really great tapas dish. The parsley and Parmesan make a fantastic topping and you'll find they are devoured the moment they are ready!

Serves 4

1 pound fresh mussels

1 tablespoon melted butter

1 tablespoon olive oil

3 tablespoons freshly grated
  Parmesan cheese

2 tablespoons chopped fresh parsley

2 garlic cloves, finely chopped

½ teaspoon coarsely ground
  black pepper

Scrub the mussels thoroughly, pulling away the gritty beards. Discard any mussels that don't close when sharply tapped with a knife.

Place the mussels and 3 tablespoons water in a large pan. Cover and steam for 5–6 minutes, until all the mussels have opened. Drain, discarding any that remain closed.

Remove and discard the top shell of each mussel. Place the mussels in a flameproof dish, packing them closely together so that they stay level. Preheat the broiler to high.

Combine the melted butter, olive oil, Parmesan, parsley, garlic, and black pepper. Spoon a little of this mixture on top of each mussel and broil for 2–3 minutes, until the mussels are sizzling and golden. Serve the mussels in their shells.

COOK'S TIP

This is a dish to serve to good friends as it can be rather messy! Remember to give guests napkins to wipe the juices off their chins.

OMELET AUX FINES HERBES

Parsley, chervil, chives, and tarragon are the four traditional ingredients in French fines herbes. *This omelet is a classic favorite and makes a welcome snack for lunch or supper.*

Serves 1

3 eggs

2 tablespoons chopped fresh parsley

2 tablespoons chopped fresh chervil

2 tablespoons chopped fresh tarragon

1 tablespoon chopped fresh chives

1 tablespoon butter

salt and freshly ground black pepper

french fries, salad greens, and

tomato, to serve

COOK'S TIP

From start to finish, an omelet should be cooked and on the table in less than a minute. For best results, use fresh eggs at room temperature.

Beat the eggs with a little salt and pepper and then whisk in the chopped parsley, chervil, tarragon, and chives.

Heat an omelet pan or skillet over high heat and add the butter. When the butter begins to foam and brown, quickly pour in the beaten egg, and stir briskly with a fork. When the egg is two-thirds scrambled, let the omelet finish cooking for a further 10–15 seconds.

Fold the omelet onto a warm serving plate. Serve with french fries, salad greens, and a halved tomato.

PARSLEY AND GARLIC MUSHROOMS

Mushrooms, parsley, and garlic have a long and happy association. The lemon juice adds a pleasant sharpness to this dish, tempering the garlic and bringing out the flavor of the parsley.

Serves 4

2 tablespoons butter, plus extra
   for spreading
1 onion, finely chopped
1 garlic clove, crushed
12 ounces assorted exotic and
   cultivated mushrooms, sliced
3 tablespoons dry sherry
5 tablespoons chopped fresh flat
   leaf parsley
1 tablespoon lemon juice
salt and freshly ground black pepper
4 slices brown or white bread

COOK'S TIP

Exotic mushrooms are becoming available in larger supermarkets or you may be lucky enough to have your own supply. Field mushrooms, shaggy ink caps, and orange birch boletes are all excellent in this dish.

Melt the butter in a large nonstick skillet and gently fry the onion until softened but not browned. Add the garlic and mushrooms, cover, and cook for 3–5 minutes. Add the sherry and cook, uncovered, for 2–3 minutes more, until the liquid has evaporated.

Stir in the parsley and lemon juice and season to taste. Toast the bread and spread with butter. Spoon the mushrooms onto the toast and serve.

MACKEREL AND PARSLEY PÂTÉ

Parsley adds flavor and color to this popular pâté. Serve it as a simple starter or snack with endive leaves and fingers of toast.

Serves 4

10 ounces smoked mackerel
*   fillet, skinned*
6 tablespoons sour cream
6 tablespoons butter, softened
2 tablespoons chopped fresh parsley
1–2 tablespoons lemon juice
freshly ground black pepper
endive leaves and parsley, to garnish
fingers of toast, to serve

COOK'S TIP
For a lower-calorie version of this rather rich pâté, substitute scant 1 cup low-fat soft cheese or strained cottage cheese for the sour cream.

Remove any skin or bones from the mackerel and then mash it with a fork. Add the sour cream and butter, blending to make a smooth paste. Stir in the parsley, lemon juice, and pepper to taste.

Spoon the pâté into a dish, cover with plastic wrap, and chill overnight.

About 30 minutes before serving, remove the pâté from the fridge and let it to return to room temperature. To serve, spoon onto individual plates and garnish with endive leaves and parsley. Serve with fingers of toast.

POTTED STILTON WITH PARSLEY

The parsley and chives give this appetizing starter a great country style flavor. It is best made the day before so that the herbs and port can blend with the Stilton. Serve with crispy Melba toast.

Serves 8

8 ounces blue Stilton or other
   blue cheese
¼ cup full- or half-fat cream cheese
1 tablespoon port
1 tablespoon chopped fresh parsley
1 tablespoon snipped fresh chives,
   plus extra to garnish
½ cup finely chopped walnuts
salt and freshly ground black pepper

For the Melba toast
12 thin slices white bread

Place the Stilton or other blue cheese, cream cheese, and port in a blender or food processor and process until smooth. Add the parsley, chives, and walnuts and season to taste with salt and pepper.

Spoon the mixture into individual ramekin dishes and level the tops. Cover with plastic wrap and chill, preferably overnight.

Just before serving, make the Melba toast. Heat the broiler and toast the bread on both sides. While the toast is still hot, cut off the crusts and cut each slice horizontally in half. Place the bread in a single layer on a broiler pan and broil for about 30 seconds, until golden brown and crisp.

Sprinkle the potted cheese with chives and serve with Melba toast.

COOK'S TIP
Take care when making Melba toast. It burns very quickly—so watch it constantly.

Meat and Poultry

Parsley enlivens stuffings and coatings and is great with all meats and poultry. From Russia, through Morocco, to England, parsley has a place in every kitchen.

BEEF STROGANOFF WITH PARSLEY

Parsley is one of the traditional ingredients in this famous nineteenth-century Russian recipe.

Serves 4

1 pound fillet steak, trimmed and cut
*   into thin strips*
2 tablespoons olive oil
3 tablespoons brandy
2 shallots, finely chopped
8 ounces chanterelle or button
*   mushrooms, trimmed and halved*
⅔ cup beef stock
5 tablespoons sour cream
1 teaspoon Dijon mustard
½ dill pickle, chopped
3 tablespoons chopped fresh parsley
salt and freshly ground black pepper
buttered noodles and poppy seeds,
*   to serve*

COOK'S TIP

To flame the brandy, heat quickly, stand back from the pan, and then tilt the pan toward the flame, or ignite with a match if cooking on an electric hob.

Season the steak with pepper. Heat half the oil in a skillet and fry the steak for 2 minutes, until evenly browned. Transfer to a large plate. Heat the skillet over moderately high heat, brown the residue, then add the brandy and ignite the alcohol vapour. Wait until the flames subside and then pour the juices over the meat. Keep warm.

Wipe the skillet and fry the shallots in the remaining oil for about 2 minutes. Add the mushrooms and fry gently for 3–4 minutes, to soften. Stir in the stock and simmer for a few minutes, then add the sour cream, mustard, and dill pickle, together with the steak and its juices. Simmer briefly, season to taste, and stir in the chopped parsley. Serve with buttered noodles sprinkled with poppy seeds.

BEEF WELLINGTON

The parsley crêpes make an unusual and tasty addition to this popular dish. The traditional goose liver pâté is replaced here with a rich mushroom pâté.

Serves 4

1½ pounds fillet steak, tied
1 tablespoon sunflower oil
12 ounces puff pastry, thawed
  if frozen
1 egg, beaten, to glaze
salt and freshly ground black pepper
watercress, to garnish

For the parsley crêpes

4 tablespoons all-purpose flour
1 egg
⅔ cup milk
2 tablespoons chopped fresh parsley

For the mushroom pâté

1 cup fresh white bread crumbs
5 tablespoons heavy cream
2 egg yolks
2 tablespoons butter
2 shallots or 1 small onion, chopped
6 cups chopped assorted exotic and
  cultivated mushrooms

Preheat the oven to 425°F and season the meat with black pepper. Heat the oil in a roasting pan, add the meat, and brown on all sides. Transfer to the oven and roast for 15 minutes for rare, 20 minutes for medium-rare, and 25 minutes for well-done meat. Set aside to cool. Reduce the oven temperature to 375°F.

Make the crêpes. Beat together the flour, a pinch of salt, the egg, milk, and parsley to make a smooth batter. Heat a large nonstick skillet and pour in enough batter to coat the base. When set, flip over, and cook briefly until lightly browned. Continue with the remaining batter to make four crêpes.

Make the mushroom pâté. Combine the bread crumbs, cream, and egg yolks. Melt the butter in a skillet and fry the shallots or onion until slightly softened. Add the mushrooms and cook briskly until the juices begin to run and then evaporate. When the mushrooms are quite dry, stir in the bread crumb mixture, blending to make a smooth paste. Let cool.

Roll out the pastry and cut into a rectangle 14 x 12 inches. Place two crêpes on the pastry and spread with mushroom pâté. Place the fillet steak on top and spread any remaining pâté over it. Cover with the remaining crêpes. Cut out four small squares from the corners of the pastry and reserve. Moisten the pastry edges and wrap over the meat.

Decorate the top with the reserved pastry trimming and transfer to a cookie sheet. Brush the pastry evenly with beaten egg and cook for about 40 minutes, until golden brown. Serve garnished with watercress.

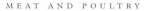

SHISH KEBAB

This is one of the most famous dishes of the Arab world and it is cooked with lots of fresh parsley. Lamb is the traditional Moroccan meat for this dish, although beef can be used.

Serves 4

1½ pounds lamb or beef

1 onion, grated

*2 tablespoons chopped fresh flat
  leaf parsley*

1 teaspoon paprika

1 teaspoon ground cumin

1 tablespoon olive oil

1 tablespoon lemon juice

salt and freshly ground black pepper

*fine strips of lemon rind and chopped
  fresh parsley, to garnish*

*Moroccan bread, lemon wedges, cumin
  seeds, and cayenne pepper, to serve*

Cut the meat into fairly small pieces, measuring approximately ¾ inch square. Combine the grated onion, parsley, paprika, cumin, oil, lemon juice, and seasoning in a large bowl and add the meat. Stir so that the meat is coated thoroughly, then set aside for about 2 hours.

Prepare a grill or preheat the broiler. Thread the meat onto metal skewers, allowing about six to eight pieces of meat per skewer. Grill or broil the meat about 1 inch from the heat for 6–8 minutes, or until the meat is cooked through, basting occasionally with the marinade. Arrange the kebabs on a serving plate and garnish with fine strips of lemon rind and chopped fresh parsley. Serve with Moroccan bread, lemon wedges, and dishes of cumin seeds and cayenne pepper.

COOK'S TIP

Moroccan cooks often intersperse lamb or beef fat with the meat, which adds flavor and keeps the meat moist. Alternatively, if using lamb, choose a more fatty cut.

Pork with Parsley Dumplings

The parsley dumplings really give this rich stew a country-style flavor. The pork is cooked with prunes and apricots—a delicious fruity combination that goes beautifully with this meat.

Serves 6

$^1/_2$ cup pitted prunes,
   roughly chopped

$^1/_2$ cup dried apricots,
   roughly chopped

$1^1/_4$ cups hard cider

2 tablespoons all-purpose flour

$1^1/_2$ pounds lean boneless pork, cubed

about 2 tablespoons sunflower oil

2 onions, roughly chopped

2 garlic cloves, crushed

6 celery stalks, roughly chopped

2 cups chicken stock

12 juniper berries, lightly crushed

2 tablespoons chopped fresh thyme

15-ounce can black-eyed
   peas, drained

salt and freshly ground black pepper

For the parsley dumplings

1 cup self-rising flour

generous $^1/_3$ cup vegetable suet

3 tablespoons chopped fresh parsley

Soak the prunes and apricots in the hard cider for 20 minutes. Preheat the oven to 350°F. Season the flour with salt and pepper and dust the pork cubes, reserving any leftover flour. Heat the oil in a large flameproof casserole and brown the meat in batches, adding a little more oil if necessary. Transfer to a plate with a slotted spoon.

Add the onions, garlic, and celery to the casserole and cook for 5–6 minutes, until the vegetables are slightly softened, stirring occasionally. Add the reserved flour and cook, stirring, for 1 minute. Blend in the stock, stirring until smooth, then add the dried fruit and cider, juniper berries, thyme, and seasoning. Bring to a boil and add the pork. Cover and cook in the oven for 50 minutes.

Just before the end of cooking, prepare the dumplings. Sift the flour into a bowl and stir in the suet and parsley. Add about 96 tablespoons water and stir to make a dough. Form into six dumplings.

Stir the peas into the casserole and adjust the seasoning. Arrange the dumplings on the stew, cover, and cook in the oven for 20–25 minutes more, until the dumplings are puffy and the pork is tender.

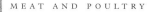

PARSLEY-CRUSTED LAMB

Parsley and oatmeal make a wonderful crunchy coating for this elegant and succulent dish.

Serves 6

*2 neck slices of lamb, about
    2¼ pounds each*
finely grated rind of 1 lemon
4 tablespoons medium oatmeal
1 cup fresh white bread crumbs
*4 tablespoons chopped fresh flat
    leaf parsley*
2 tablespoons butter, melted
2 tablespoons clear honey
salt and freshly ground black pepper
fresh parsley sprigs, to garnish
roasted baby vegetables, to serve

COOK'S TIP

*Ask the butcher to remove the
chine bone for you, which will
make carving easier. Racks of
lamb sold in supermarkets are
normally "chined" already.*

Preheat the oven to 400°F. Trim the racks of lamb so that about 1 inch of bone at the top is exposed. Trim the skin and some of the fat from the outer side of the rack and score with a sharp knife.

Combine the lemon rind, oatmeal, bread crumbs, chopped parsley, and seasoning and stir in the melted butter. Brush the fatty side of each rack with honey and press the oatmeal mixture evenly onto the surface.

Place the racks in a roasting pan with the oatmeal sides uppermost. Roast for 40–50 minutes, depending on whether you like rare or medium lamb. Cover loosely with foil if browning too much. To serve, slice each rack into three and arrange on warm serving plates with roasted vegetables, garnished with parsley sprigs.

CHICKEN WITH PARSLEY STUFFING

These little chicken drumsticks have a delectable herb flavor, in which parsley predominates.

Serves 4

4 tablespoons ricotta cheese

1 garlic clove, crushed

2 tablespoons chopped fresh parsley

1 tablespoon mixed chopped fresh
chives and tarragon

1 teaspoon mint

2 tablespoons fresh brown
bread crumbs

8 chicken drumsticks

8 smoked bacon slices

1 teaspoon wholegrain mustard

1 tablespoon sunflower oil

salt and freshly ground black pepper

chopped fresh parsley and chives,
to garnish

COOK'S TIP

*If, thanks to the elements, you
can't use the grill, cook indoors
in a preheated oven at 350°F
for 25–30 minutes, turning
occasionally.*

Combine the ricotta, garlic, herbs, bread crumbs, and seasoning. Carefully loosen the skin of each drumstick and spoon a little of the herb stuffing under the skin. Smooth the skin firmly over the stuffing.

Wrap a bacon slice around the wide end of each drumstick, to hold the skin in place over the stuffing.

Combine the mustard and oil and brush the chicken with the mixture. Cook over a medium-hot grill for about 25 minutes, turning occasionally, until the chicken is cooked through and the meat juices run clear. Serve garnished with chopped parsley and chives.

CHICKEN FRICASSÉE FORESTIER

Chicken, exotic mushrooms, and lavish quantities of parsley make this a truly splendid dish, perfect for a special meal, yet surprisingly easy and quick to make.

Serves 4

3 boneless chicken breasts, sliced

1 tablespoon sunflower oil

4 tablespoons butter

¾ cup chopped unsmoked bacon

5 tablespoons dry sherry or white
   wine

1 onion, chopped

5 cups sliced assorted exotic and
   cultivated mushrooms

3 tablespoons all-purpose flour

2¼ cups chicken stock

2 teaspoons lemon juice

4 tablespoons chopped fresh parsley

salt and freshly ground black pepper

boiled rice, carrots, and baby corn,
   to serve

COOK'S TIP

It is worth spending a little extra on high-quality chicken for the low fat content and good flavor and texture of the meat.

Season the chicken with a little pepper. Heat the oil and half of the butter in a large skillet or flameproof casserole and brown the chicken and bacon pieces. Transfer to a dish and pour away any excess fat. Return the skillet to the heat and brown the residue. Pour in the sherry or wine, stir with a wooden spoon to deglaze the skillet, and then pour the liquid over the chicken. Wipe the skillet clean.

Fry the onion in the remaining butter until golden brown. Add the mushrooms and cook, stirring frequently, for 6–8 minutes. Reduce the heat, stir in the flour, and then gradually add the chicken stock, stirring to make a smooth sauce.

Add the reserved chicken and bacon, together with the sherry juices and heat until simmering. Simmer for 10–15 minutes, until the chicken is cooked, then add the lemon juice, parsley (reserve a little parsley to scatter over the rice if you wish), and seasoning. Serve with plain boiled rice, carrots, and baby corn.

CHICKEN, LEEK, AND PARSLEY PIE

This is a classic English country dish. The creamy parsley sauce is the perfect complement to the chicken and leeks, bound together in an exquisite whole with wonderful melt-in-the-mouth pastry.

Serves 4–6

3 part-boned chicken breasts

flavoring ingredients (bouquet garni, black peppercorns, onion and carrot)

4 tablespoons butter

2 leeks, thinly sliced

1/2 cup grated Cheddar cheese

1/3 cup grated Parmesan cheese

3 tablespoons chopped fresh parsley

2 tablespoons wholegrain mustard

1 teaspoon cornstarch

1 1/4 cups heavy cream

salt and freshly ground black pepper

beaten egg, to glaze

salad greens, to serve

For the pastry

2 1/2 cups all-purpose flour

scant 1 cup butter, diced

2 egg yolks

pinch of salt

Make the pastry. Sift the flour and salt into a bowl. Process the butter and egg yolks in a food processor until creamy. Add the flour and process very briefly until the mixture is just coming together. Add about 1 tablespoon cold water and process for a few seconds more. Turn out onto a lightly floured surface and knead lightly. Wrap in plastic wrap and chill for about 1 hour.

Meanwhile, place the chicken breasts in a single layer in a skillet. Add the flavoring ingredients and enough water just to cover. Cover the skillet with a lid and simmer very gently for about 20–25 minutes, until the chicken is tender. Let cool in the liquid.

Preheat the oven to 400°F. Divide the pastry into two pieces, one slightly larger than the other. Roll out the larger piece on a lightly floured surface and use to line an 11 x 7 inch ovenproof dish or pan. Prick the base with a fork and bake in the oven for 15 minutes. Let cool.

Discard the skin and bones from the chicken and cut the flesh into strips. Melt the butter in a skillet and fry the leeks over low heat until soft, stirring occasionally. Stir in the cheeses and parsley. Spread half the leek mixture onto the cooked pastry base, cover with the chicken strips, and then top with the remaining leek mixture. Combine the mustard, cornstarch, and cream in a small bowl. Add seasoning to taste and pour onto the filling.

Moisten the edges of the cooked pastry base. Roll out the remaining pastry and cover the pie. Brush with beaten egg and bake for 30–40 minutes, until crisp and golden. Serve hot with salad greens.

Fish and Seafood

*Its mild, pleasant flavor makes parsley
an essential ingredient when cooking with fish.
Sauces, risottos, and tasty fish soups would be
incomplete without this fresh green herb.*

FISH STEW WITH PARSLEY

This rustic stew harbors all sorts of tantalizing flavors, enhanced by aromatic flat leaf parsley.

Serves 4

2¼ pounds assorted white fish fillets

*8 ounces button mushrooms, halved
   if large*

8 ounces canned tomatoes

1¾ cups hard cider

2 teaspoons all-purpose flour

1 tablespoon butter

3 tablespoons Calvados

*1 tablespoon chopped fresh flat
   leaf parsley*

1 tablespoon chopped fresh dill

salt and freshly ground black pepper

*fresh flat leaf parsley sprigs and dill,
   to garnish*

Preheat the oven to 350°F. Chop the fish roughly and place in a casserole with the mushrooms and tomatoes. Heat the hard cider in a small pan. Work the flour into the butter and stir, one piece at a time, into the cider to make a smooth sauce. Remove the pan from the heat.

Stir in the Calvados, chopped parsley and dill and season to taste with salt and pepper. Pour into the casserole with the fish and mushrooms, cover, and cook in the oven for about 30 minutes, until the fish is tender. Serve garnished with parsley sprigs and dill.

CRAB PATTIES WITH PARSLEY SAUCE

These crab patties are served with a tartar-like sauce, richly flavored with onions, capers, and parsley.

Serves 4

1½ pounds fresh crab meat

1 egg, beaten

2 tablespoons mayonnaise

1 tablespoon Worcestershire sauce

1 tablespoon dry sherry

*2 tablespoons finely chopped
   fresh parsley*

*1 tablespoon finely chopped fresh
   chives or dill*

3 tablespoons olive oil

salt and freshly ground black pepper

*chives, slices of lemon, and salad
   greens, to garnish*

For the parsley sauce

1 egg yolk

1 tablespoon white wine vinegar

2 tablespoons Dijon mustard

1 cup sunflower oil

2 tablespoons lemon juice

2 scallions, finely chopped

2 tablespoons drained capers, chopped

3–4 dill pickles, finely chopped

3 tablespoons chopped fresh parsley

Place the crab meat in a bowl, discarding any pieces of shell but keeping the pieces of crab as large as possible.

Put the egg, mayonnaise, Worcestershire sauce, sherry, and chopped herbs in a bowl and stir to mix. Season with salt and pepper, then fold in the crab meat. Divide the mixture into eight oval patties and place on a cookie sheet between layers of waxed paper. Chill for at least 1 hour.

Meanwhile, make the sauce. Using a wire whisk, beat the egg yolk and add the vinegar, mustard, and seasoning. Whisk in the oil, at first drop by drop, and then in a slow, steady stream, to make a smooth mayonnaise. Add the lemon juice, scallions, capers, dill pickles, and parsley and mix well. Adjust the seasoning, cover, and chill.

Preheat the broiler. Brush the crab patties with the olive oil and place on an oiled cookie sheet. Broil under a moderately hot heat for about 5 minutes each side, until golden brown. Serve hot with the parsley sauce, garnished with chives, lemon slices, and a few salad greens.

SEAFOOD RISOTTO WITH PARSLEY

Parsley and chervil add color and a pleasant, aromatic flavor to this tasty risotto. Use short-grain risotto rice which has a creamy texture to complement the shellfish and mushrooms.

Serves 4

8 ounces fresh mussels

3 tablespoons olive oil

1 onion, chopped

3 cups sliced assorted exotic and
   cultivated mushrooms

2¼ cups risotto rice

5 cups boiling chicken or
   vegetable stock

⅔ cup white wine

4 ounces shrimp, shelled

8 ounces clams

1 squid, cleaned, trimmed, and sliced

5 tablespoons mixed chopped fresh
   flat leaf parsley and chervil

celery salt and cayenne pepper

Scrub the mussels thoroughly, pulling away the gritty beards. Discard any mussels that don't close when sharply tapped with a knife. Heat the oil in a large skillet and fry the onion for 6–8 minutes, until softened but not browned. Add the mushrooms and cook for 5–6 minutes, stirring occasionally. Add the rice and cook for about 1 minute to coat the rice in oil, then pour in the stock and wine. Add the shrimp, mussels, clams, and squid and simmer for 15 minutes, stirring occasionally. Discard any shellfish that have not opened during cooking.

Add the herbs, stir well, then remove from the heat. Cover tightly and let stand for 5–10 minutes, until the rice is completely tender. Season with celery salt and cayenne pepper to taste, and serve.

COOK'S TIP
Be sure to discard any uncooked mussels that do not close when sharply tapped.

PARSLEY-STUFFED FLOUNDER ROLLS

Sun-dried tomatoes, pine nuts, and plenty of flat leaf parsley make an appetizing stuffing with a superb southern European flavor.

Serves 4

4 flounder fillets, about 8 ounces
  each, skinned
6 tablespoons butter
1 small onion, chopped
1 celery stalk, finely chopped
2 cups fresh white bread crumbs
3 tablespoons chopped fresh flat
  leaf parsley
2 tablespoons pine nuts, toasted
3–4 sun-dried tomatoes in oil,
  drained and chopped
2-ounce can anchovy fillets, drained
  and chopped
5 tablespoons hot fish stock
freshly ground black pepper

Preheat the oven to 350°F. Using a sharp knife, cut the flounder fillets in half lengthwise to make eight smaller fillets. Melt the butter in a pan. Add the onion and celery and cook, covered, over very low heat for about 15 minutes, until they are both very soft. Combine the bread crumbs, parsley, pine nuts, sun-dried tomatoes, and anchovies in a bowl. Stir in the softened vegetables and buttery juices and season to taste with freshly ground black pepper.

Divide the stuffing into eight portions and form each one into a small ball. Roll this up inside a flounder fillet, securing each roll with a toothpick.

Place the rolled-up fillets in a buttered ovenproof dish. Pour in the fish stock, cover with buttered foil, and bake for about 20 minutes, until the fish flakes easily. Remove the toothpicks and serve with a little of the cooking juices drizzled on top.

COOK'S TIP
This dish is superb served with baby new potatoes topped with a pat of butter.

HADDOCK AND PARSLEY SAUCE

Parsley sauce is a classic with white fish, but it is excellent with smoked fish too. Add lots of parsley and season well so that the sauce stands up to the smoky flavor of the fish.

Serves 4

4 smoked haddock fillets, about
   8 ounces each
6 tablespoons butter, softened
2 tablespoons all-purpose flour
1¼ cups milk
4 tablespoons chopped fresh parsley
salt and freshly ground black pepper
fresh parsley sprigs, to garnish

COOK'S TIP

You could use flat leaf or curly parsley for this dish. Flat leaf parsley has the more aromatic flavor, but curly parsley is also very good and would be the traditional variety to serve with this British dish.

Smear the fish fillets on both sides with 4 tablespoons of the butter and preheat the broiler. Beat the remaining butter and flour together to make a thick paste.

Broil the fish for 10–15 minutes, turning when necessary. Meanwhile, heat the milk until just below boiling point. Add the flour mixture in small pieces, whisking constantly over the heat. Continue until you have used all the flour mixture and the sauce is smooth and thick.

Stir in the parsley and season well to taste. Pour on the fish, garnish with parsley, and serve.

SOLE IN A PARSLEY JACKET

Quick to prepare and absolutely delicious, there is nothing to compare with the rich sweetness of sole. The parsley adds a subtle flavor, as well as looking magnificent.

Serves 2

2 sole, skinned

2 tablespoons butter

salt and freshly ground black pepper

lemon wedges, halved cherry
*   tomatoes, and fresh flat leaf*
*   parsley sprigs, to garnish*

mashed potatoes, to serve

For the parsley jacket

1 cup fresh flat leaf parsley

1 thick crustless slice white bread,
*   about 1 ounce, cubed*

3 tablespoons milk

2 tablespoons olive oil

finely grated rind of 1/2 small lemon

2 small garlic cloves, crushed

First make the parsley jacket. Place the parsley in a food processor and process until finely chopped. Add the bread, milk, olive oil, lemon rind, and garlic and process to make a fine paste.

Preheat a moderate broiler. Season the fish, dot with butter, and broil for 5 minutes. Turn and broil for 2 minutes on the other side. Spread this side with the parsley mixture and cook under the broiler for another 5 minutes, until the fish flakes easily. Garnish the fish with lemon wedges, tomato halves, and parsley and serve with creamy mashed potatoes.

SPANISH-STYLE HAKE WITH PARSLEY

This is essentially a main meal soup. Fish, mussels, and green beans make the substance of the soup, while the stock is flavored with wine, sherry, and lots of lovely parsley.

Serves 4

16–20 fresh mussels

2 tablespoons olive oil

2 tablespoons butter

1 onion, chopped

3 garlic cloves, crushed

1 tablespoon all-purpose flour

1/2 teaspoon paprika

4 hake cutlets, about 6 ounces each

8 ounces fine green beans, cut into
   1-inch lengths

1 1/2 cups fish stock

2/3 cup dry white wine

2 tablespoons dry sherry

3 tablespoons chopped fresh parsley

salt and freshly ground black pepper

crusty bread, to serve

COOK'S TIP
Cod and haddock cutlets will work just as well in this tasty dish.

Scrub the mussels thoroughly, pulling away the gritty beards. Discard any mussels that don't close when sharply tapped with a knife. Heat the oil and butter in a skillet and fry the onion for 5 minutes, until softened but not browned. Add the crushed garlic and cook for 1 minute more.

Combine the flour and paprika and lightly dust the hake cutlets. Push the onion and garlic to one side of the skillet and add the fish. Fry on both sides until golden, then carefully stir in the beans, stock, wine, sherry, and seasoning. Bring to a boil and cook for about 2 minutes.

Add the prepared mussels and parsley, cover the skillet, and cook for 5–8 minutes, until the mussels have opened. Discard any mussels that remain closed.

Serve this dish in warm, shallow soup bowls with crusty bread to mop up the juices.

Vegetable Dishes

Parsley is the perfect herb for subtle vegetable dishes. Whether used in sauces, stirred into stuffings, or starring in salads, this versatile herb adds vibrant color with its unassuming but much-loved flavor.

STUFFED PARSLEY ONIONS

The tasty parsley stuffing goes perfectly with roasted onions. Serve as part of a vegetarian meal or as an accompaniment to roast meat or chicken.

Serves 4

4 large onions

4 tablespoons cooked rice

4 teaspoons finely chopped fresh parsley, plus extra to garnish

4 tablespoons freshly grated Cheddar cheese

2 tablespoons olive oil

about 1 tablespoon white wine, to moisten

salt and freshly ground black pepper

COOK'S TIP

The onion centers can be used in soups or for other dishes. However, uncooked cut onion does not keep well, so use on the same day or discard.

Preheat the oven to 350°F. Cut a slice from the top of each onion and scoop out the center, leaving a fairly thick shell. Combine the cooked rice, parsley, grated cheese, olive oil, and seasoning, moistening with enough wine to mix well.

Fill the onions and bake for 45 minutes. Serve garnished with a sprinkling of chopped parsley.

53

PARSLEYED VEGETABLE RIBBONS

Brie and parsley combine to make a delicately flavored sauce to serve with these elegant vegetables.

Serves 4

1 tablespoon sunflower oil

*1 large green bell pepper, cored
    and diced*

8 ounces Brie cheese

2 tablespoons crème fraîche

1 teaspoon lemon juice

4 tablespoons milk

*2 teaspoons freshly ground
    black pepper*

2–3 fresh parsley sprigs

6 large zucchini

6 large carrots

chopped fresh parsley, to garnish

Heat the oil in a pan and sauté the bell pepper for 4–5 minutes, until just tender. Place the Brie, crème fraîche, lemon juice, milk, black pepper, and parsley sprigs in a food processor and process well. Add the mixture to the bell pepper and heat gently.

Using a potato peeler, slice the zucchini and carrots into thin strips. Place them in separate saucepans with enough water to cover and simmer for 3 minutes, until just tender. The zucchini will take 2–3 minutes, the carrots a little longer. Drain.

Pour the warm sauce into a shallow serving dish. Add the zucchini and carrots and toss carefully to coat in the sauce. Garnish with a little finely chopped parsley and serve.

LEEKS WITH PARSLEY DRESSING

The parsley dressing gives these leeks a wonderful flavor. Serve French-style as a salade tiède *(warm salad), with broiled or poached fish and new potatoes.*

Serves 4
1¹/₂ pounds young leeks

For the dressing
1 cup fresh flat leaf parsley
2 tablespoons olive oil
juice of ¹/₂ lemon
¹/₂ cup broken walnuts, toasted
1 teaspoon superfine sugar
1 hard-cooked egg, shelled
salt and freshly ground black pepper

Cut the leeks into 4-inch lengths and rinse well to remove any grit or soil. Bring a saucepan of salted water to a boil and simmer the leeks for 8 minutes. Drain and rinse well in cold water to cool slightly, and then drain again thoroughly.

Make the dressing. Reserve a sprig or two of parsley for the garnish and put the remainder in a blender or food processor. Process until finely chopped, add the olive oil, lemon juice, and toasted walnuts and process again for 1–2 minutes, until smooth. Add about 6 tablespoons water to make a smooth sauce and add sugar and seasoning to taste.

Arrange the leeks on a serving plate and spoon on the sauce. Finely grate the hard-cooked egg and scatter on the sauce. Serve at room temperature, garnished with the reserved parsley.

PARSLEY AND ARTICHOKE CRÊPES

Fill thin crêpes with a mouthwatering soufflé mixture of Jerusalem artichokes, leeks, and chopped fresh parsley to serve for a special main course.

Serves 4

1 cup all-purpose flour

pinch of salt

1 egg

1¼ cups milk

For the soufflé filling

*1 pound Jerusalem artichokes, peeled
    and diced*

1 large leek, thinly sliced

4 tablespoons butter

2 tablespoons self-rising flour

2 tablespoons light cream

¾ cup grated Cheddar cheese

2 tablespoons fresh parsley, chopped

fresh nutmeg, grated

2 eggs, separated

COOK'S TIP

*Make sure the pan is at a good
steady heat and is well oiled
before you pour in the batter. It
should sizzle as it hits the pan.*

Make the crêpe batter. Process the flour, salt, egg, and milk to a smooth batter in a food processor or blender. Using a crêpe or omelet pan with a diameter of about 8 inches, make a batch of thin crêpes. You will need about 2 tablespoons of batter for each one. Stack the crêpes under a dish cloth as you make them. Reserve eight for this dish and freeze the rest.

Cook the artichokes and leek with the butter in a covered saucepan over low heat for about 12 minutes, until very soft. Mash with the back of a wooden spoon. Season well. Stir the flour into the vegetables and cook for 1 minute more. Take the pan off the heat and beat in the cream, cheese, parsley, and nutmeg. Season to taste. Cool, then add the egg yolks.

Whisk the egg whites until they form soft peaks and carefully fold them into the leek and artichoke mixture. Lightly grease a small ovenproof dish and preheat the oven to 375°F. Fold each crêpe in four, hold the top open, and spoon the mixture into the center. Arrange the crêpes in the prepared dish with the filling uppermost if possible. Bake for about 15 minutes, until risen and golden. Serve immediately.

BEANS WITH PARSLEY SAUCE

In this classic dish, the parsley sauce is enriched with egg yolks and heavy cream.

Serves 4

1½ tablespoons butter

2–2½ pounds fresh fava
  beans, shelled

1 large fresh parsley sprig

⅔ cup heavy cream

3 egg yolks

a few drops of lemon juice

2 tablespoons chopped fresh parsley

salt and freshly ground black pepper

Melt the butter in a saucepan and stir in the beans. Cook for 2–3 minutes, then add the parsley sprig, seasoning, and enough water just to cover the beans. Cover the pan tightly, bring to boiling point, and then immediately lower the heat and cook very gently for 15–20 minutes, shaking the pan occasionally, until the beans are tender and no liquid remains. Remove the pan from the heat, discard the parsley, and let cool slightly.

Combine the cream and egg yolks and stir into the beans. Reheat gently, stirring constantly, until the sauce coats the back of the spoon: do not boil.

Add a few drops of lemon juice and adjust the seasoning. Sprinkle with the chopped parsley and serve.

COOK'S TIP

If the beans are not as fresh as you would like and if you have the time and patience, slip off the outer skin of each bean. The bright green inner bean is wonderfully sweet and tender.

BAKED SQUASH IN PARSLEY SAUCE

This creamy parsley sauce is a really glorious way of enriching a simple and modest vegetable.

Serves 4

1 small young summer squash,
    about 2 pounds
2 tablespoons olive oil
1 tablespoon butter
1 onion, chopped
1 tablespoon all-purpose flour
1¼ cups milk and light
    cream, mixed
2 tablespoons chopped fresh parsley
salt and freshly ground black pepper

COOK'S TIP
If desired, remove the lid for the final 5 minutes of cooking to gratinize the top of the dish.

Preheat the oven to 350°F and cut the squash into rectangular pieces, about 2 x 1 inch. Heat the oil and butter in a flameproof casserole and fry the onion over low heat until very soft. Add the squash and sauté for 1–2 minutes, then stir in the flour. Cook for a few minutes and stir in the milk and cream mixture.

Add the parsley and seasoning and stir well to mix. Cover and cook in the oven for 30–35 minutes. Serve hot.

FENNEL TABBOULEH WITH PARSLEY

Tabbouleh is famous for using huge quantities of fresh parsley. Here fennel adds a lovely aniseed flavor, while the pomegranate gives a tantalizing sweetness.

Serves 6

1 cup bulgur wheat

1 pomegranate

2 fennel bulbs

1 small fresh red chili, seeded and finely chopped

1 celery stalk, finely sliced

2 tablespoons olive oil

finely grated rind and juice of 2 lemons

6–8 scallions, chopped

6 tablespoons chopped fresh mint

6 tablespoons chopped fresh parsley

salt and freshly ground black pepper

Soak the bulgur wheat in enough cold water to cover for 30 minutes. Drain through a strainer, pressing out any excess water using the back of a spoon. Scoop out the pomegranate seeds and place in a large bowl. Halve the fennel bulbs, cut into very fine slices, and add to the pomegranate seeds with the chili, celery, olive oil, lemon rind and juice, scallions, mint, and parsley. Add the bulgur wheat and seasoning and stir well. Cover and let stand for 30 minutes before serving.

PASTA RAPIDO WITH PARSLEY PESTO

Here's a fresh, lively sauce to perk up pasta. It's similar to traditional pesto, but uses almonds instead of pine nuts and parsley instead of basil.

Serves 4

1 pound dried pasta

³/₄ cup whole almonds

¹/₂ cup slivered almonds

1¹/₂ cups fresh flat leaf parsley

2 garlic cloves, crushed

3 tablespoons olive oil

3 tablespoons lemon juice

1 teaspoon sugar

¹/₃ cup freshly grated
    Parmesan cheese

COOK'S TIP

The other half of the sauce will keep in a screw-topped jar in the fridge for up to 10 days.

Cook the pasta in plenty of boiling salted water according to the instructions on the packet. Toast the whole and slivered almonds separately under a moderate broiler until golden brown.

Place the parsley in a food processor and finely chop. Add the whole almonds and process again until very finely chopped. Add the garlic, olive oil, lemon juice, sugar and 1 cup boiling water. Blend to a smooth sauce. Drain the pasta and combine with half of the sauce. Top with Parmesan cheese and toasted slivered almonds.

GNOCCHI WITH PARSLEY SAUCE

A mushroom and parsley sauce brings an exquisite flavor to these Italian potato dumplings.

Serves 4

1 pound peeled mealy potatoes

1 pound peeled pumpkin, chopped

2 egg yolks

about 1¾ cups all-purpose flour

pinch of ground allspice

¼ teaspoon ground cinnamon

pinch of grated nutmeg

finely grated rind of ½ orange

⅔ cup Parmesan cheese shavings

salt and freshly ground black pepper

For the sauce

2 tablespoons olive oil

1 shallot

1⅓ cups sliced chanterelles or
*   oyster mushrooms*

2 teaspoons butter

⅔ cup crème fraîche

a little milk or water

5 tablespoons chopped fresh parsley

Cook the potatoes in simmering salted water for about 20 minutes, until tender. Drain and set aside. Place the pumpkin in a bowl, cover, and microwave on full power for 8 minutes. Alternatively, wrap the pumpkin in foil and bake at 350°F for 30 minutes. Drain well, add to the potatoes, and then pass through a vegetable mill into a bowl. Add the egg yolks, flour, spices, orange rind, and seasoning and mix to make a soft dough, adding more flour if the mixture is too soft.

Bring a large pan of salted water to a boil and dredge a counter with all-purpose flour. Spoon the gnocchi mixture into a pastry bag fitted with a ½-inch plain tip. Pipe onto the floured counter to make a 6-inch sausage. Roll in flour and cut into 1-inch pieces. Repeat the process, making more sausage shapes. Mark each lightly with a fork and cook for 3–4 minutes in the boiling water. If cooking in batches, keep the gnocchi warm in a covered dish while cooking the remainder.

Make the sauce. Heat the oil in a nonstick skillet and fry the shallot until softened but not browned. Add the mushrooms, cook briefly, and then add the butter. Stir to melt and stir in the crème fraîche. Simmer briefly and adjust the consistency with milk or water. Add the parsley and season to taste with salt and pepper.

Lift the gnocchi out of the water with a slotted spoon and place in warm soup bowls. Spoon on the sauce and scatter with Parmesan cheese shavings. Serve immediately.

INDEX